Slugdala!

13 banana slug mandalas

by Ryan Forsythe

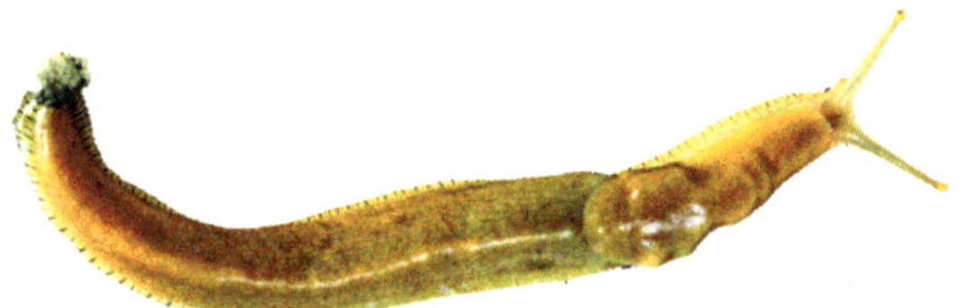

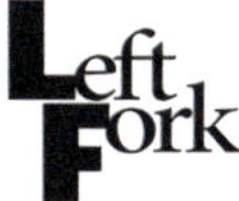

Left Fork

All images copyright © 2015 Ryan Forsythe

First Left Fork edition November 2015
ISBN 978-0-692-37998-1
No banana slugs were harmed in the making of this book

Banana Slug *What*?

Banana slug mandalas, of course!

Mandala is a Sanskrit word which can be loosely translated as *circle*. In Hinduism and Buddhism, the mandala is a spiritual and ritual symbol representing wholeness. It's something of a geometric diagram reminding us of our relationship to the universe. It may seem odd to form such cosmic designs with images of banana slugs, but then again these animals are an integral part of the circle of life in the forests where I live.

How did it come about that I found myself making abstract art out of these funny little *Ariolimax*? (Yup, that's the genus for the three species of banana slugs.) It began when my wife Kaci and I were living in Santa Cruz, California. One of my work colleagues had graced the walls of the staff break room with the art of his own nature mandalas. So, yes, you could say I stole outright the concept (thanks, Michael!). Though perhaps by focusing exclusively on banana slugs, I've given a unique perspective on the mandalas.

Of course it hasn't escaped my notice that Santa Cruz is home to a university whose very mascot is the Banana Slug, though I must admit I didn't actually create my first slugdala until we moved from town. Before I perfected my mandala-making skills, Kaci and I left Santa Cruz to manage a hostel in Redwood National Park. We got a fancy camera, and, after noticing that those giant Redwoods didn't look nearly as impressive when printed on my 4" x 6" photographs (or before me in exciting 72 dots per inch on my computer), I turned my attention to something considerably smaller.

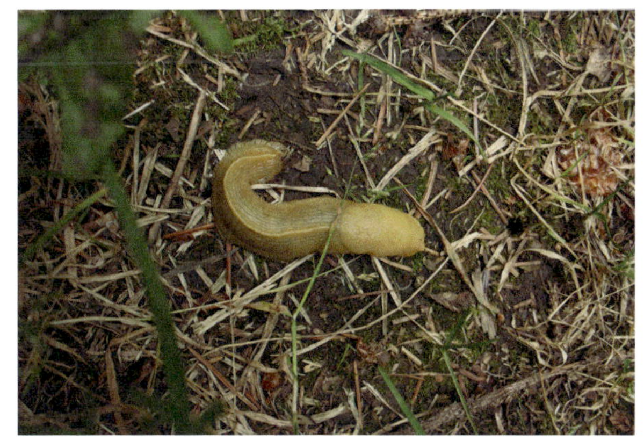

The banana slug.

How Now Slugdala?

So how do I do I make the mandalas out of the slug images? Or rather, how can anyone create their own nature mandalas? The process begins by highlighting and cropping a triangular section of the original image. So for the image on the previous page, we might get something like this:

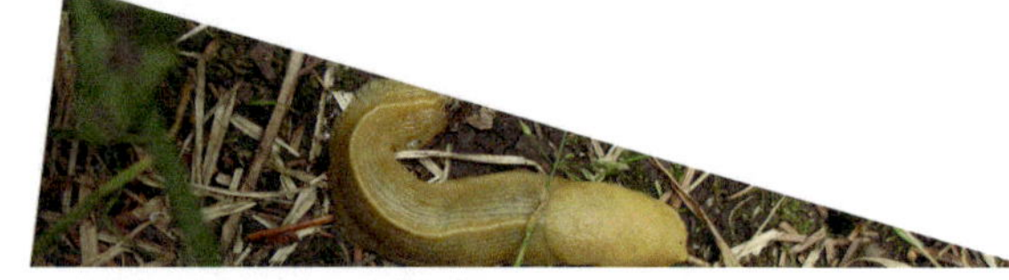

Next, make a copy of this wedge, so you have two of them. Invert the second image and move it so the slice is joined to its mirror image. This forms one "spoke" of the final mandala, as seen below right.

By continuing to add spokes to the original, and rotating each slightly, eventually it reaches a full 360 degrees. On the next page, you can see the end result of joining several of these particular spokes. Incidently, the last "slugdala" in the book also began with this very same slug image, though I highlighted a different slice of the original photograph.

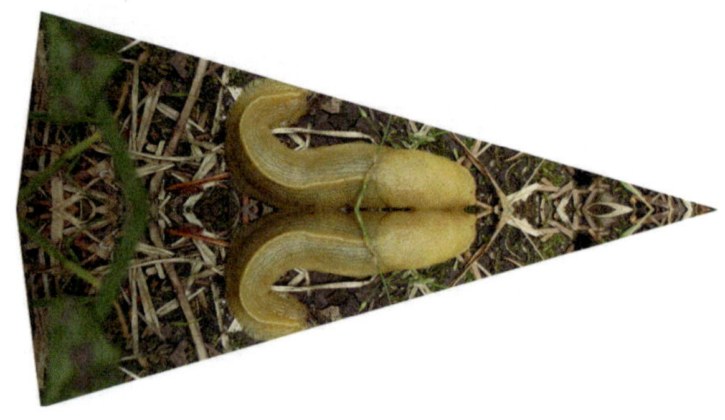

This is the basic idea, though over time I've made a number of variations to the process, as you may notice in the following pages. The end result is an interesting mix of the natural and the abstract. Thank you for taking a gander at these, though I encourage you to try your hand at your own nature mandalas.

-Ryan Forsythe

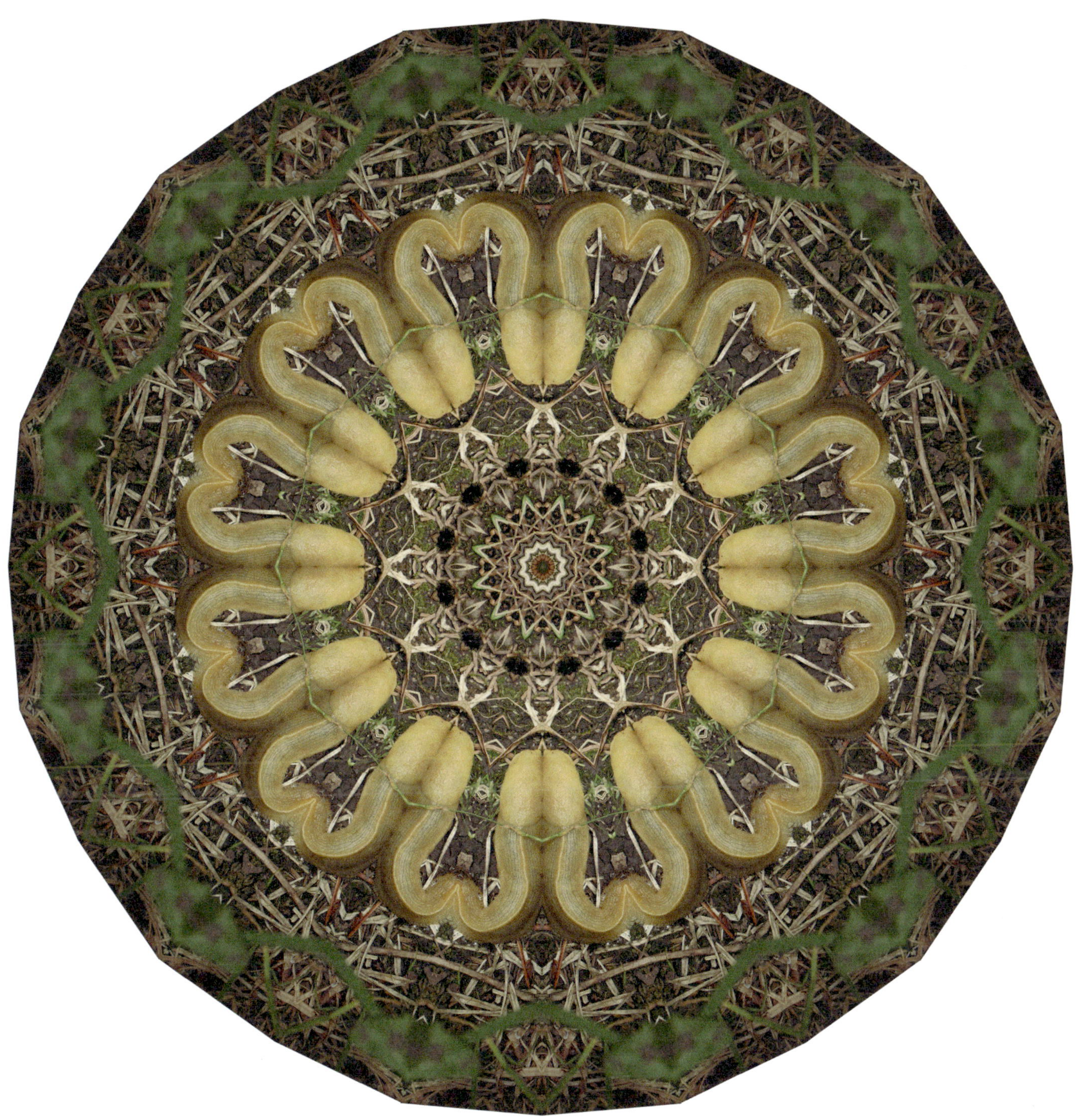

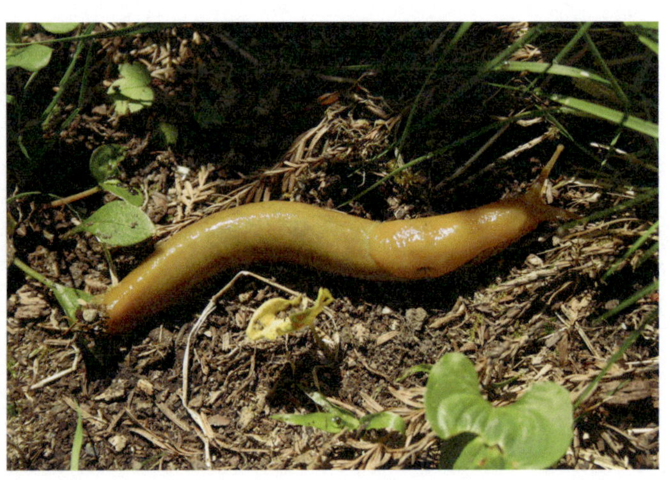

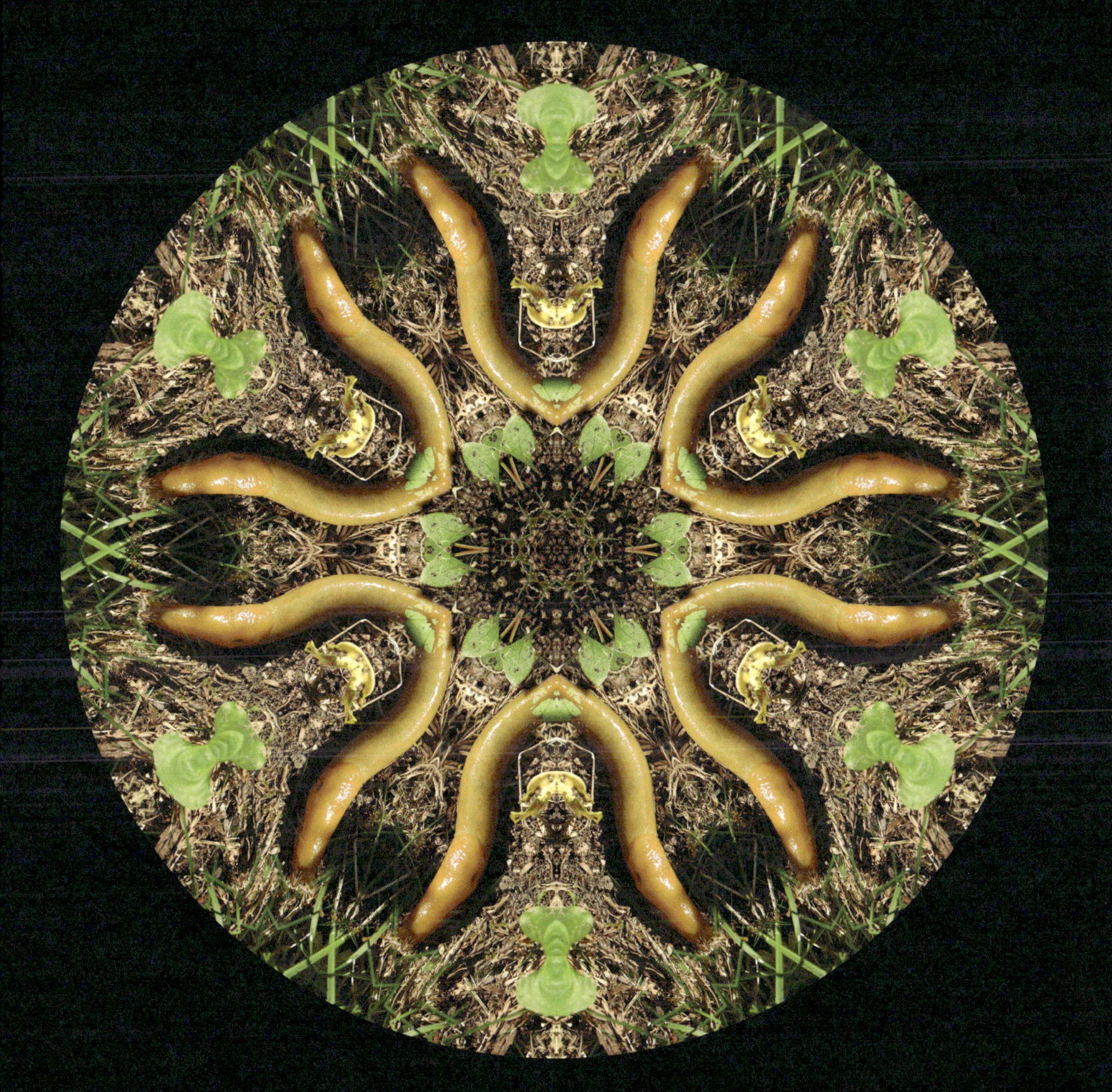

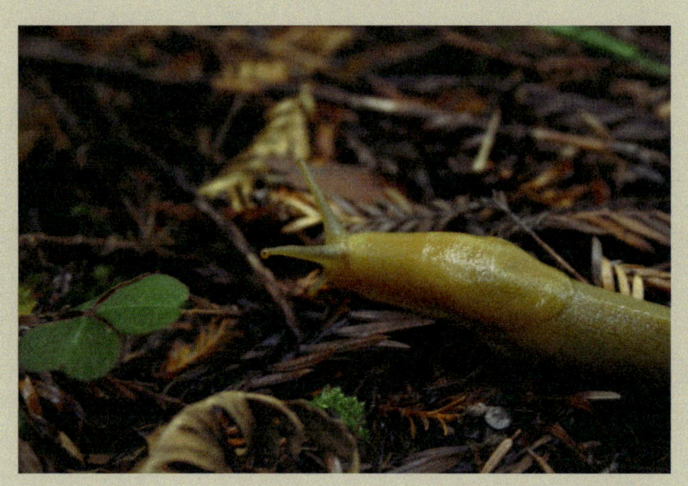

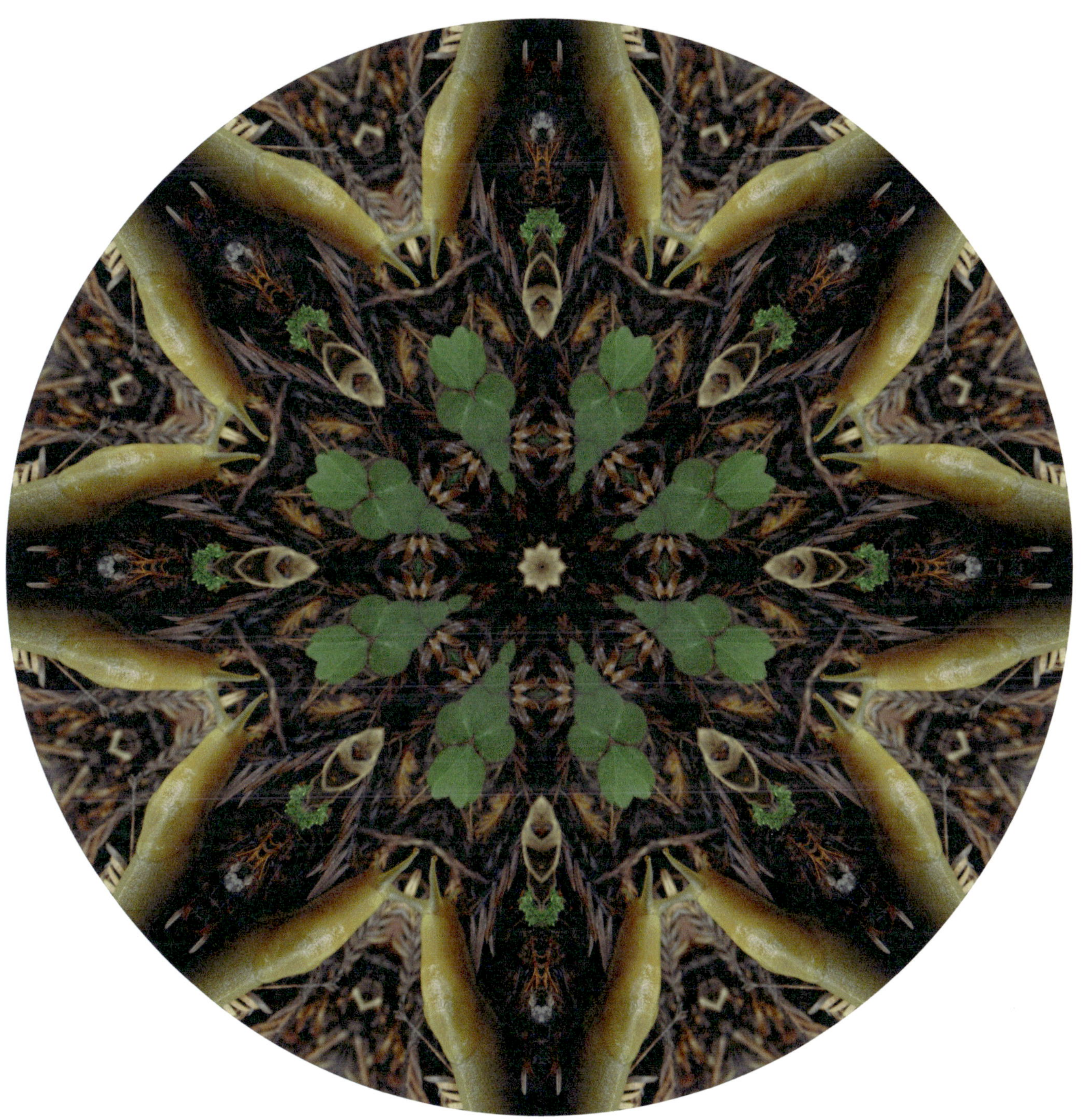

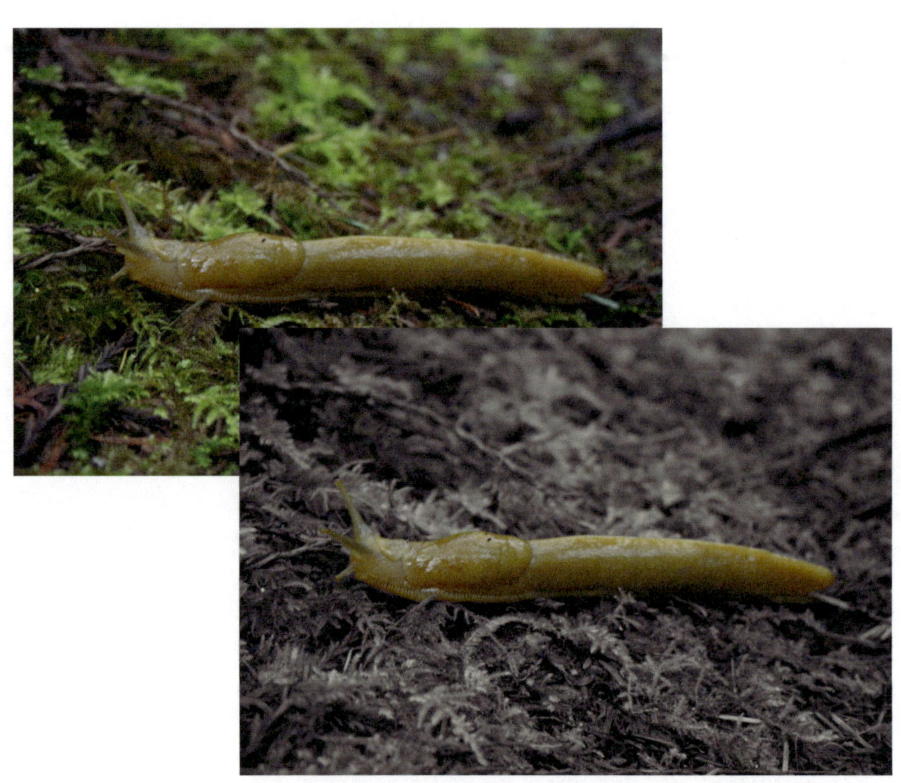

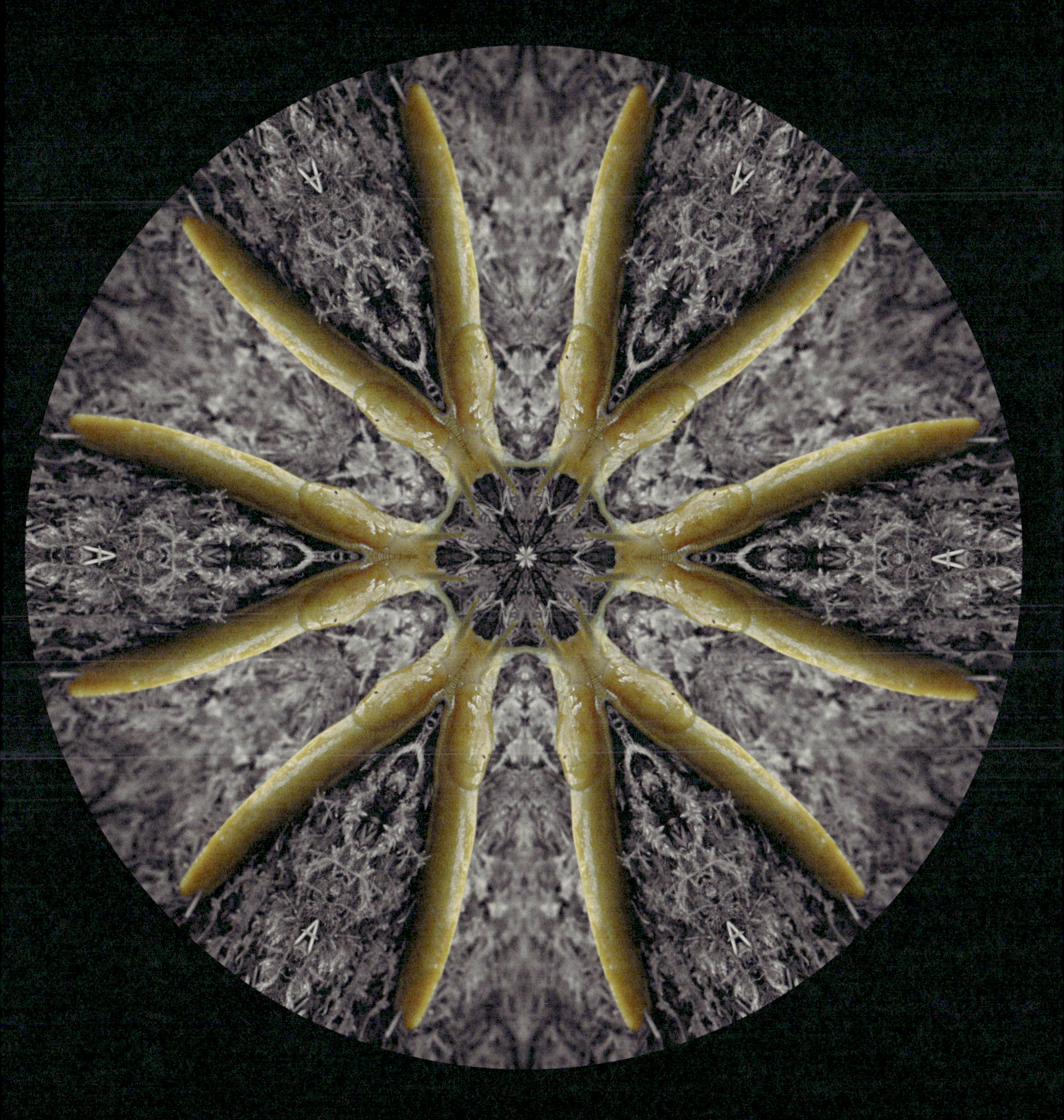

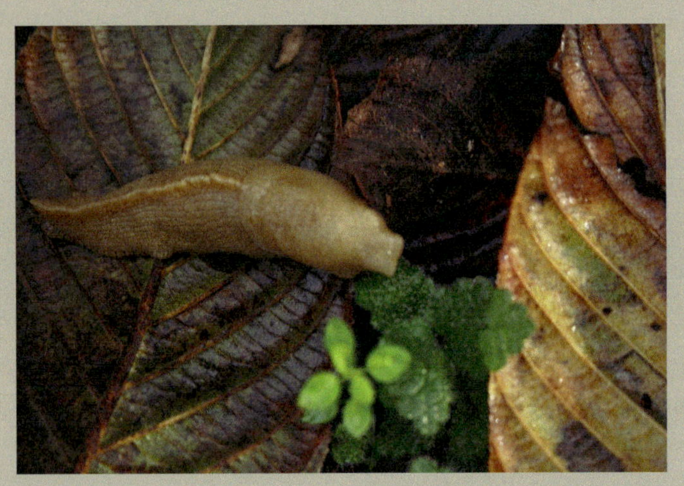

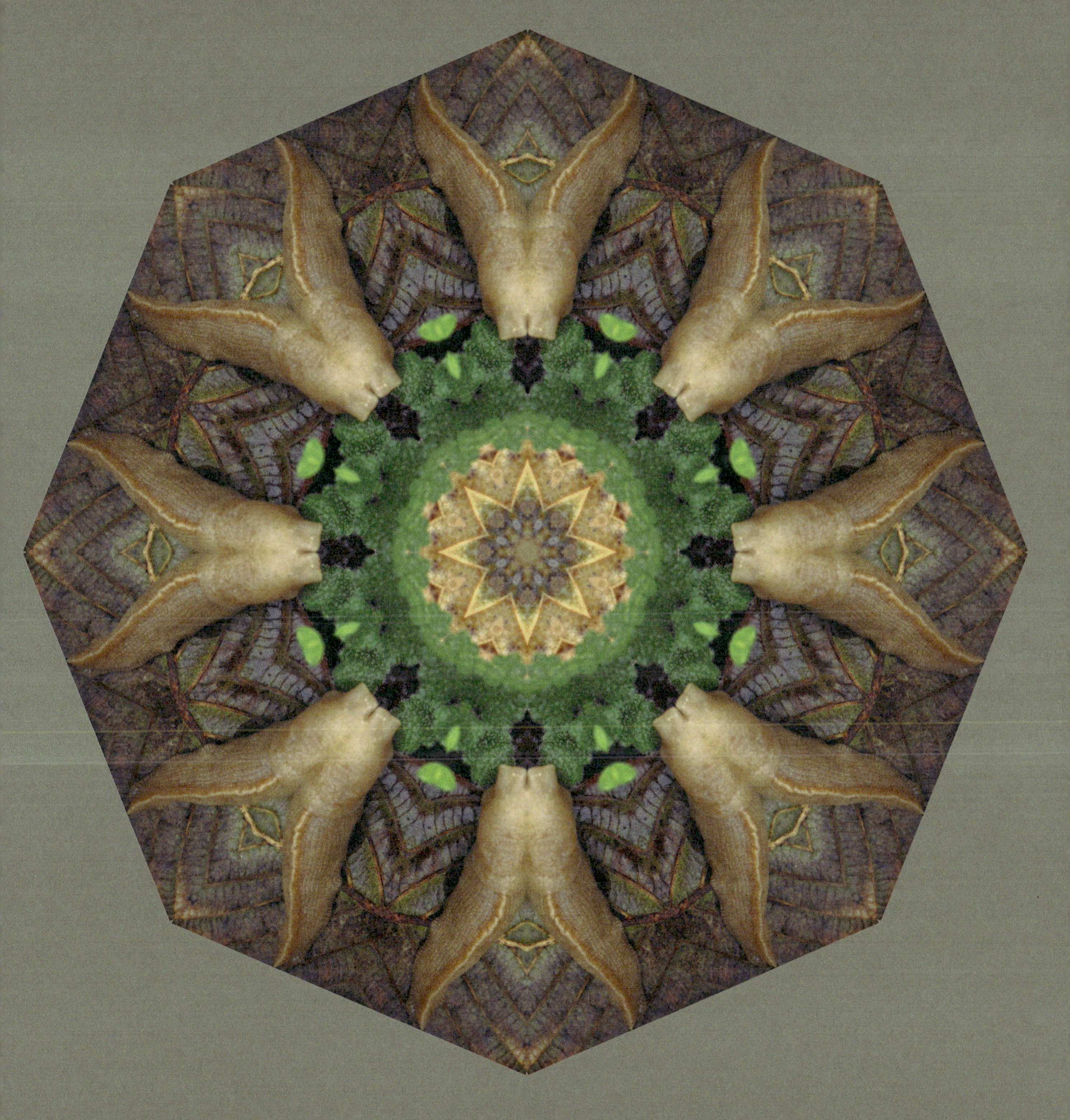

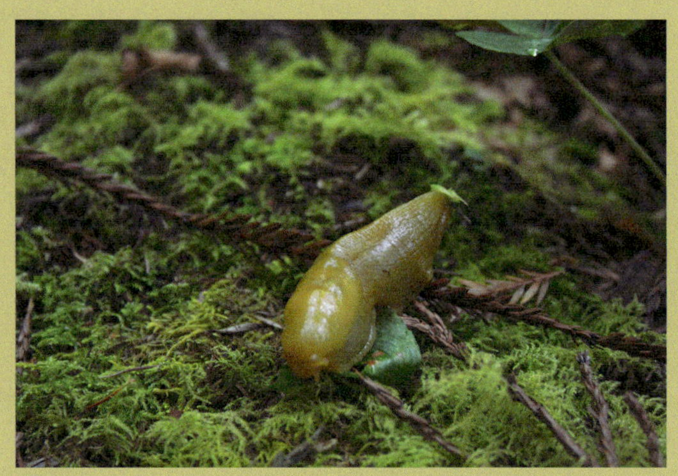

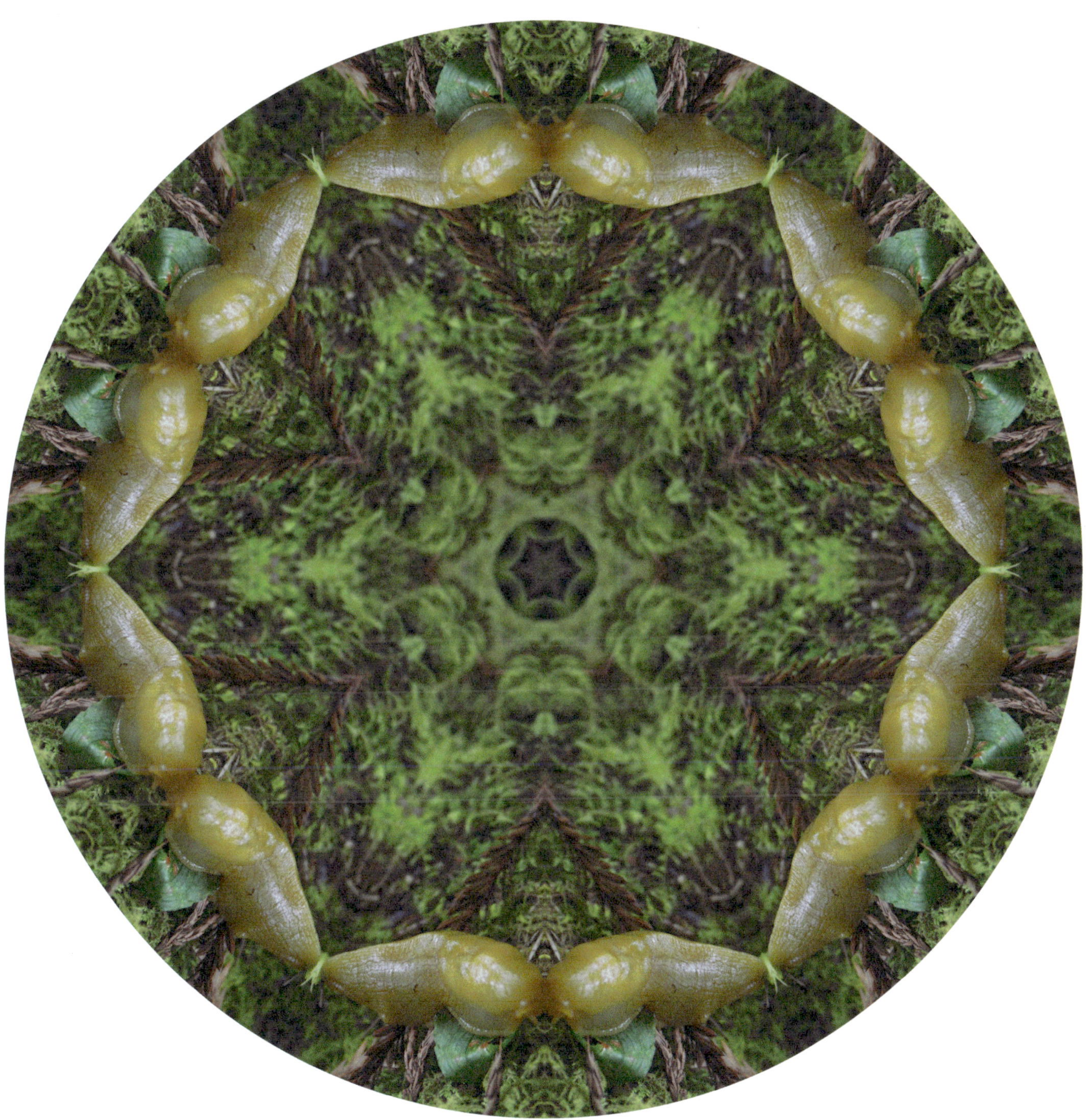

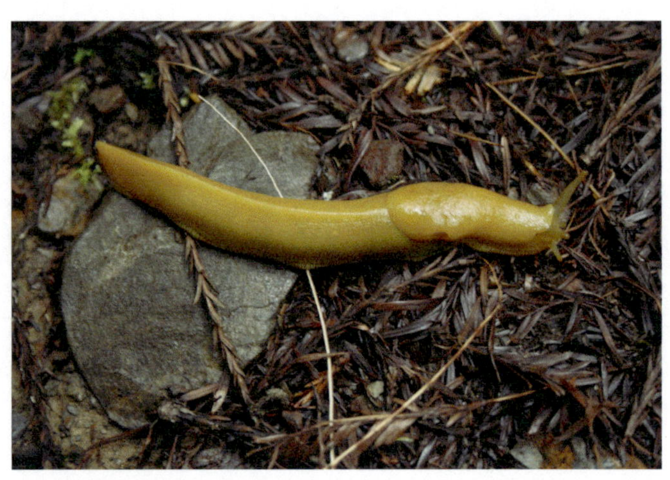

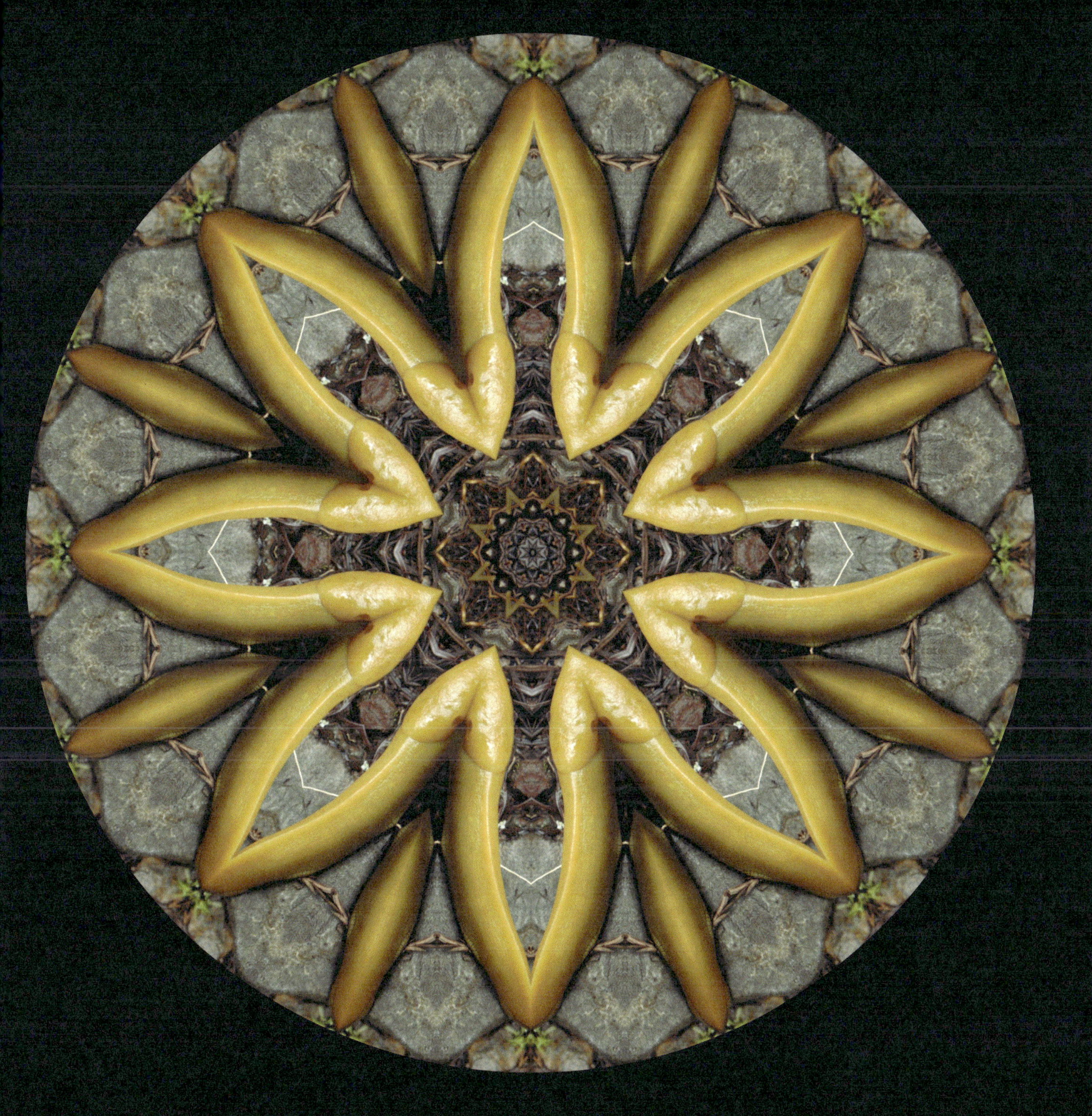

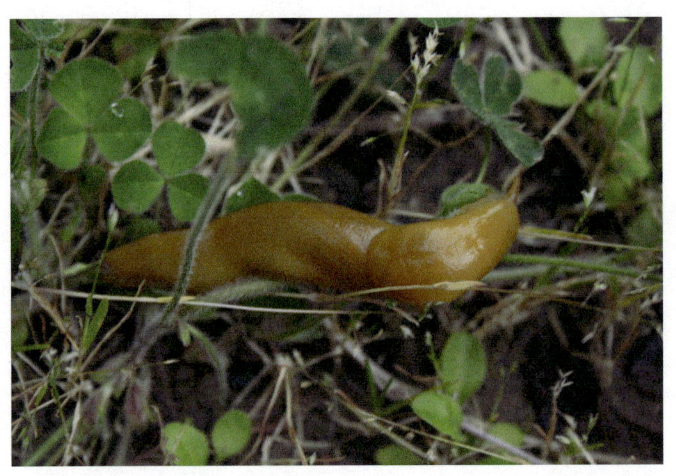

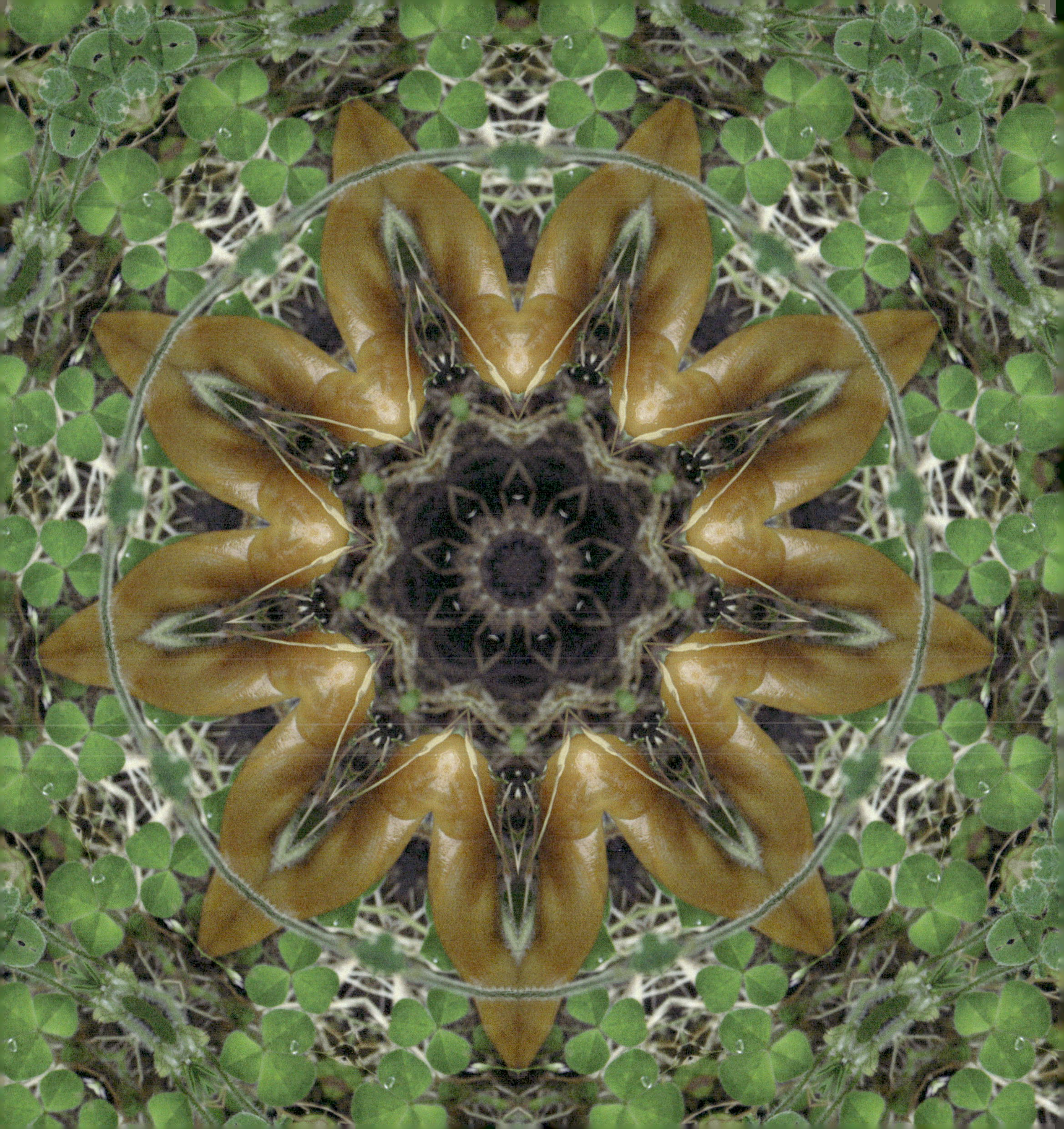

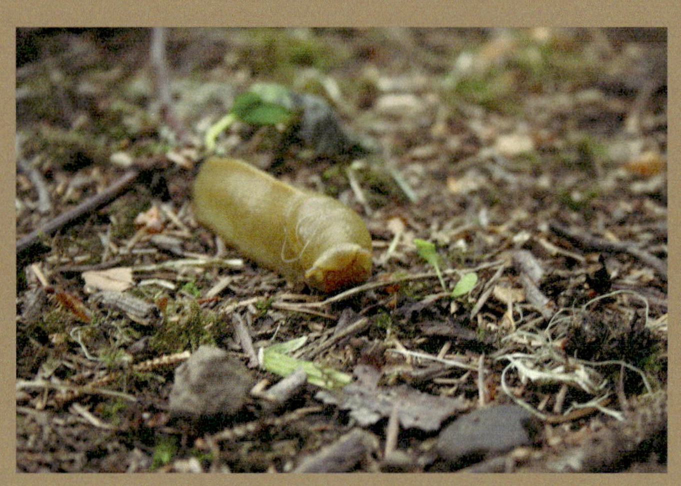

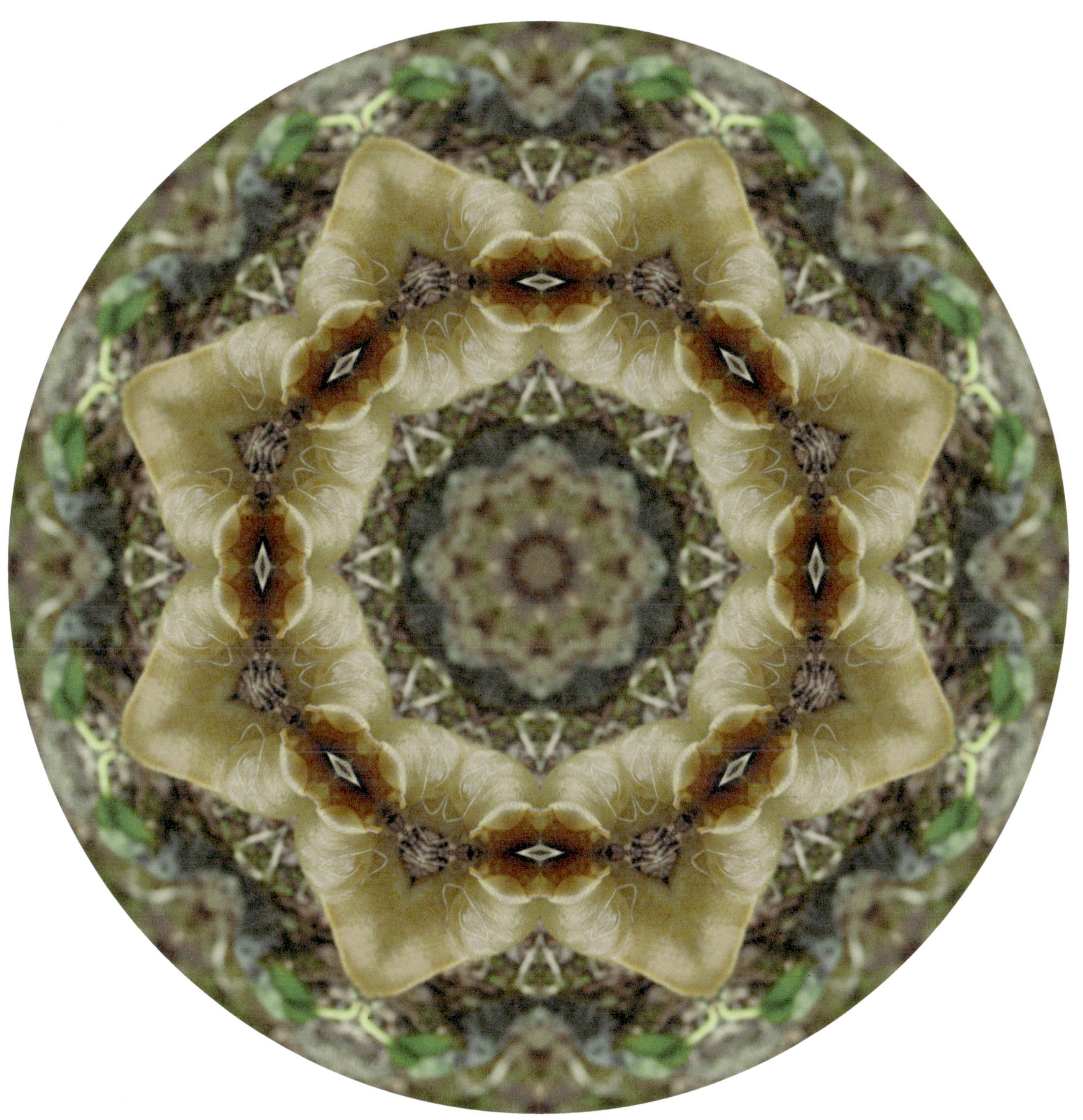

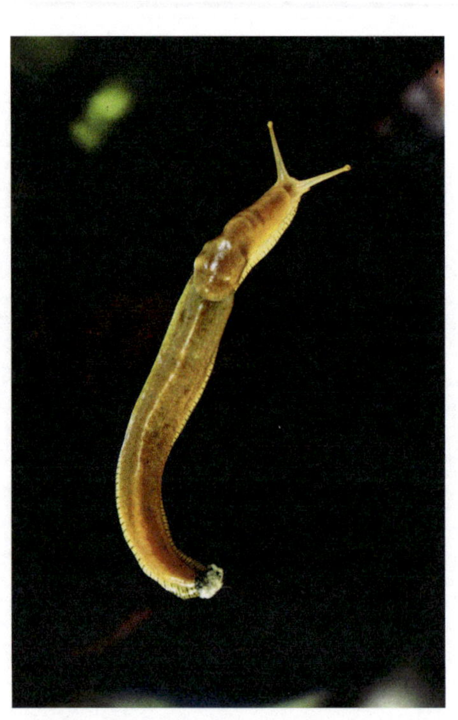

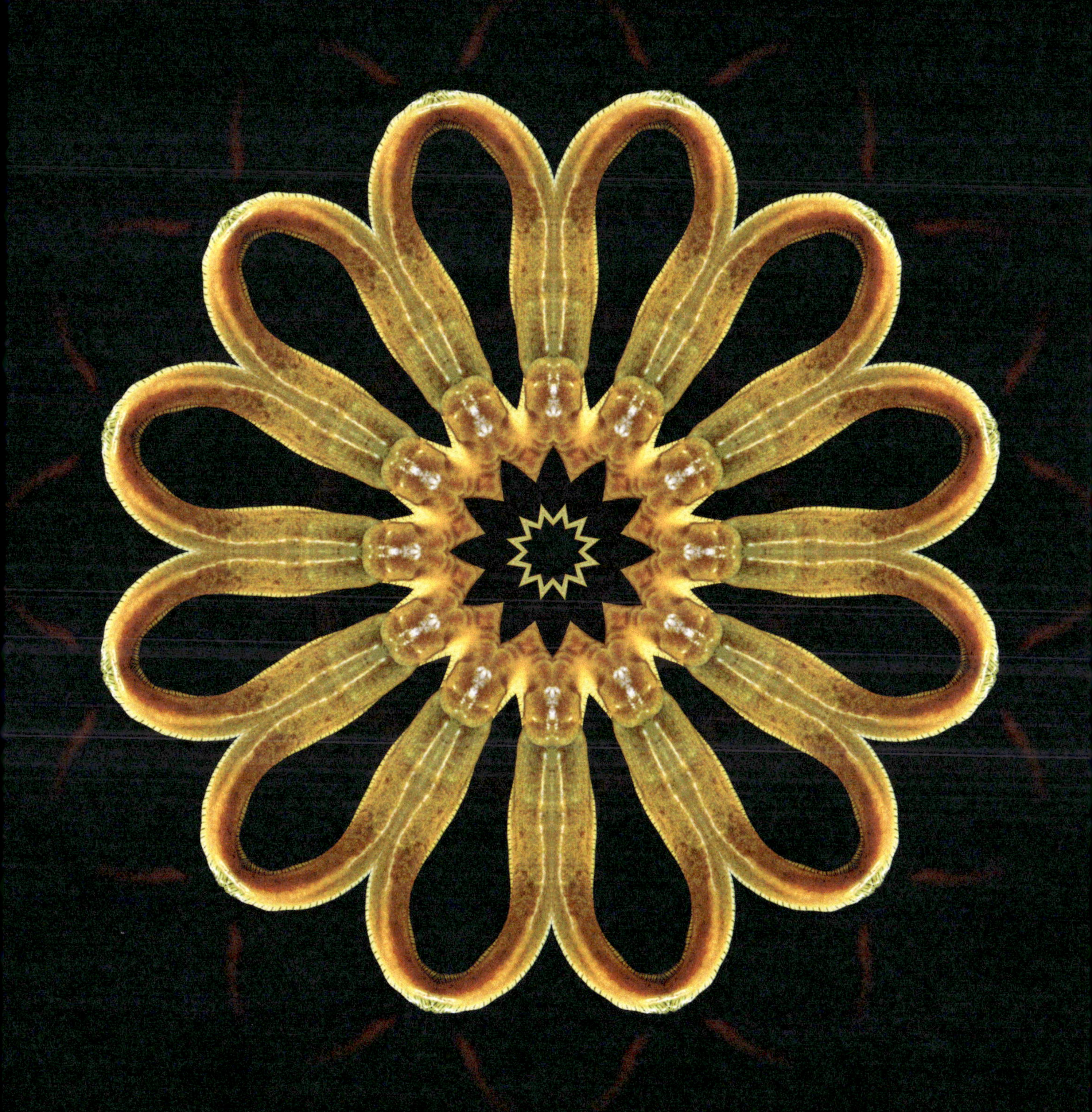

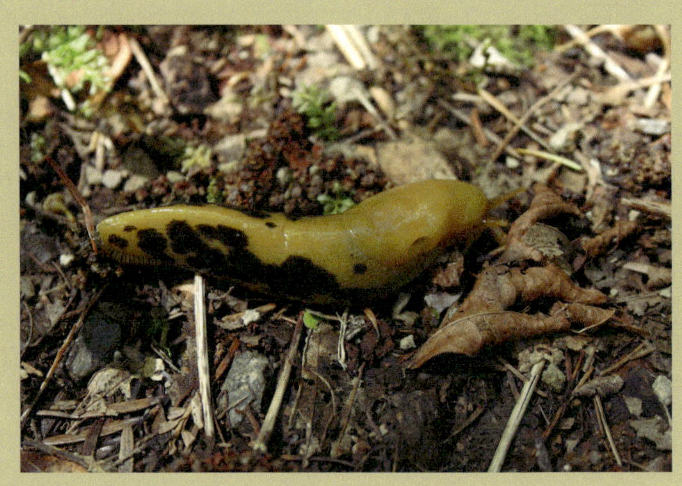

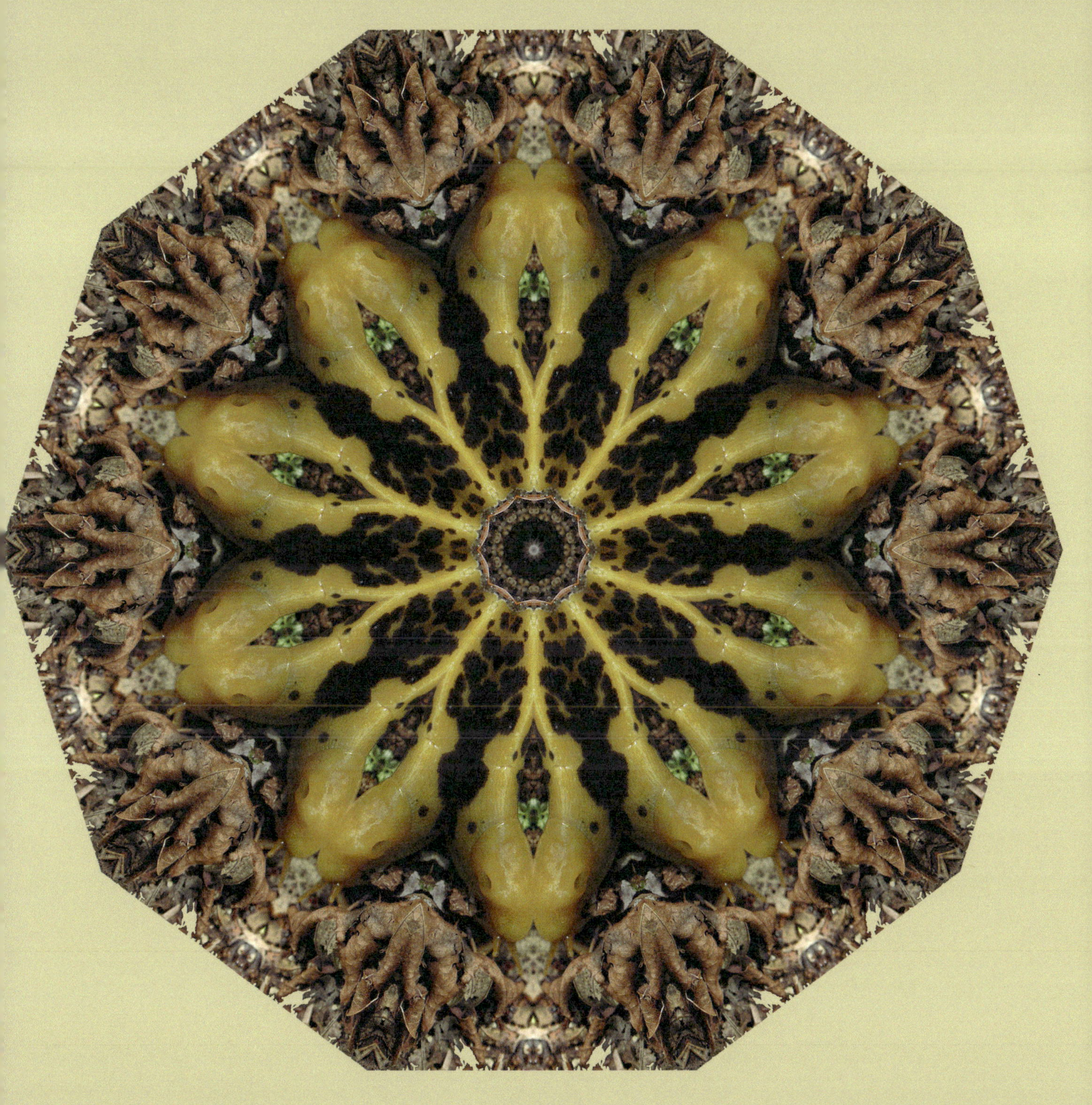

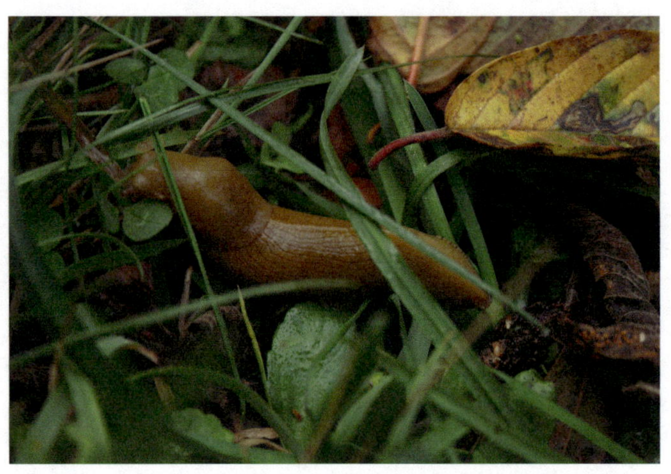

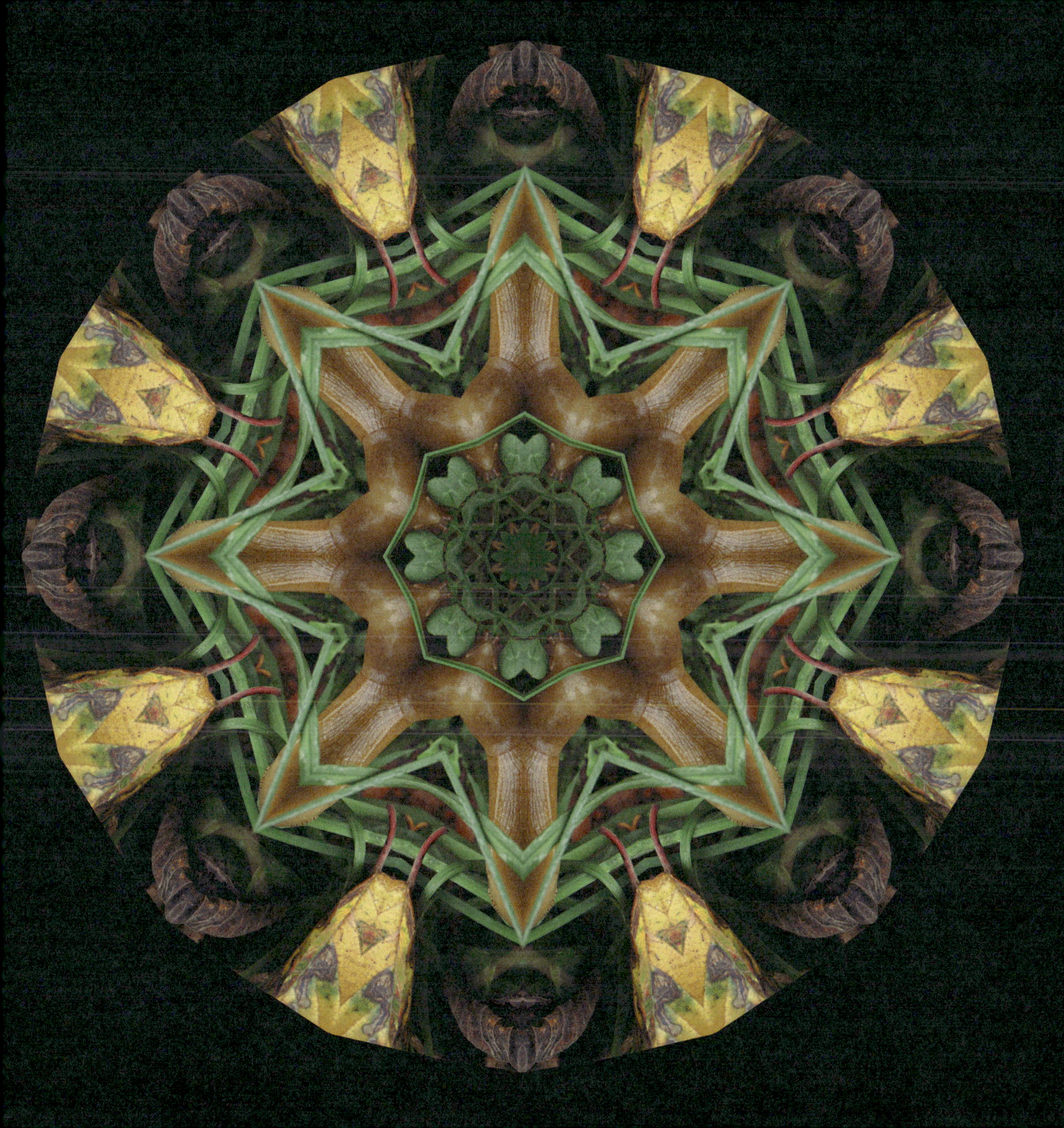

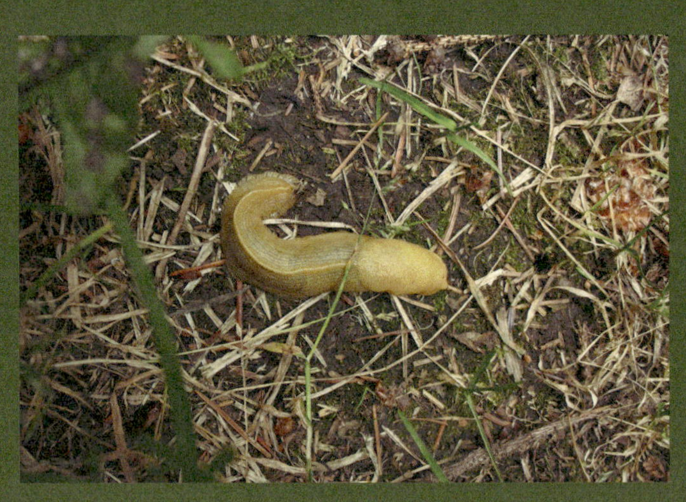

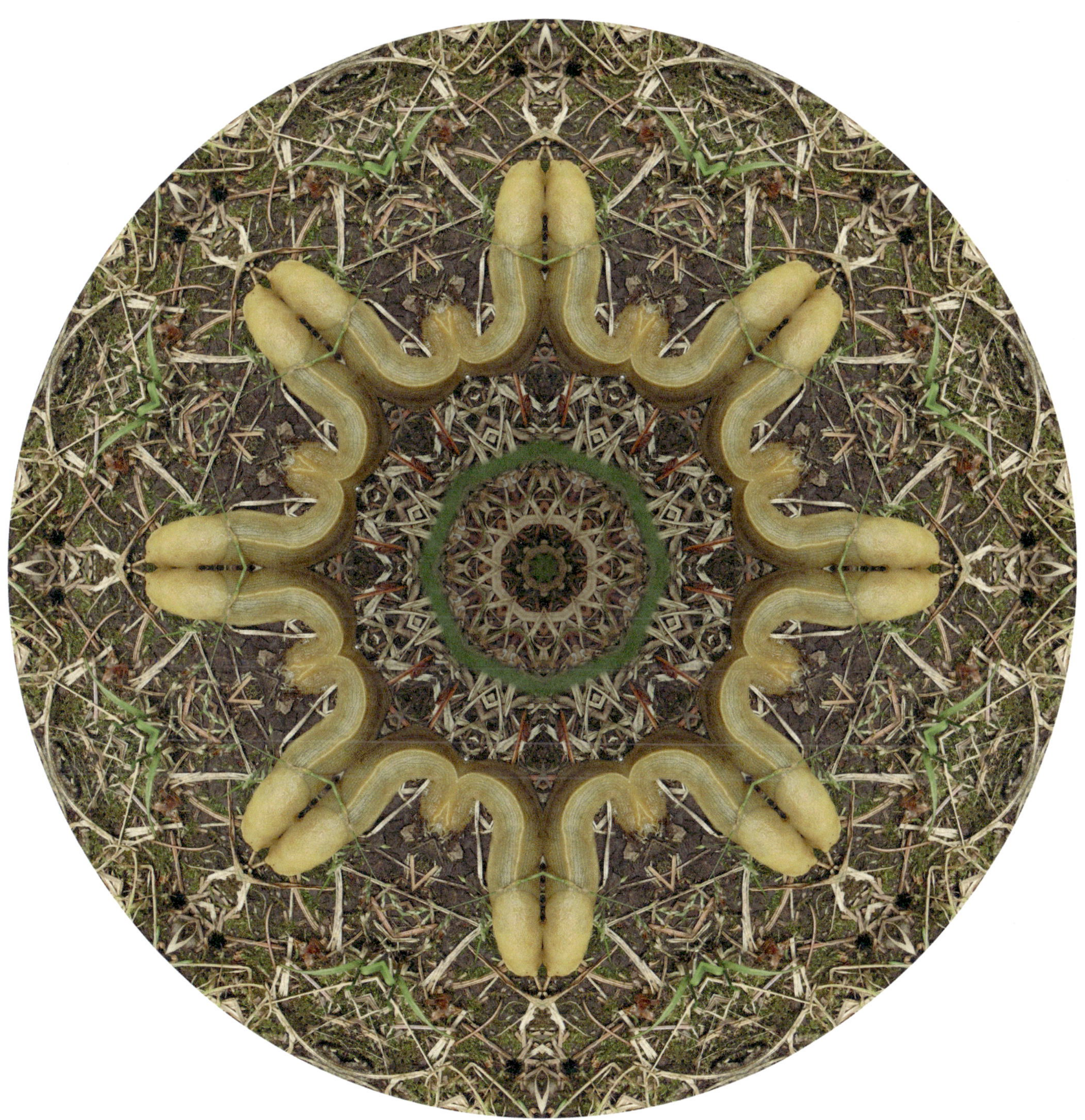

Made in the USA
Monee, IL
07 July 2026

56551685R00019